Wonders

Mc
Graw
Hill
Education

Cover and Title Page: Nathan Love

www.mheonline.com/readingwonders

Mc Graw Hill

Copyright © 2017 McGraw-Hill Education

Send all inquiries to:
McGraw-Hill Education
2 Penn Plaza
New York, NY 10121

ISBN: 978-0-02-130675-6
MHID: 0-02-130675-3

Printed in the United States of America.

4 5 6 7 8 9 LKV 28 27 26 25   C

Wonders

ELD
Companion Worktext

Program Authors

Diane August

Jana Echevarria

Josefina V. Tinajero

Mc Graw Hill Education

Discoveries

The Big Idea

Discoveries

The BIG Idea

How can discoveries open up new possibilities?

Weekly Concept Myyths

? Essential Question

Why do people tell and retell myths?

>> *Go Digital*

4

Who is the man in the photo dressed up to be? What details about his face are important? Write words and phrases in the chart about the photo.

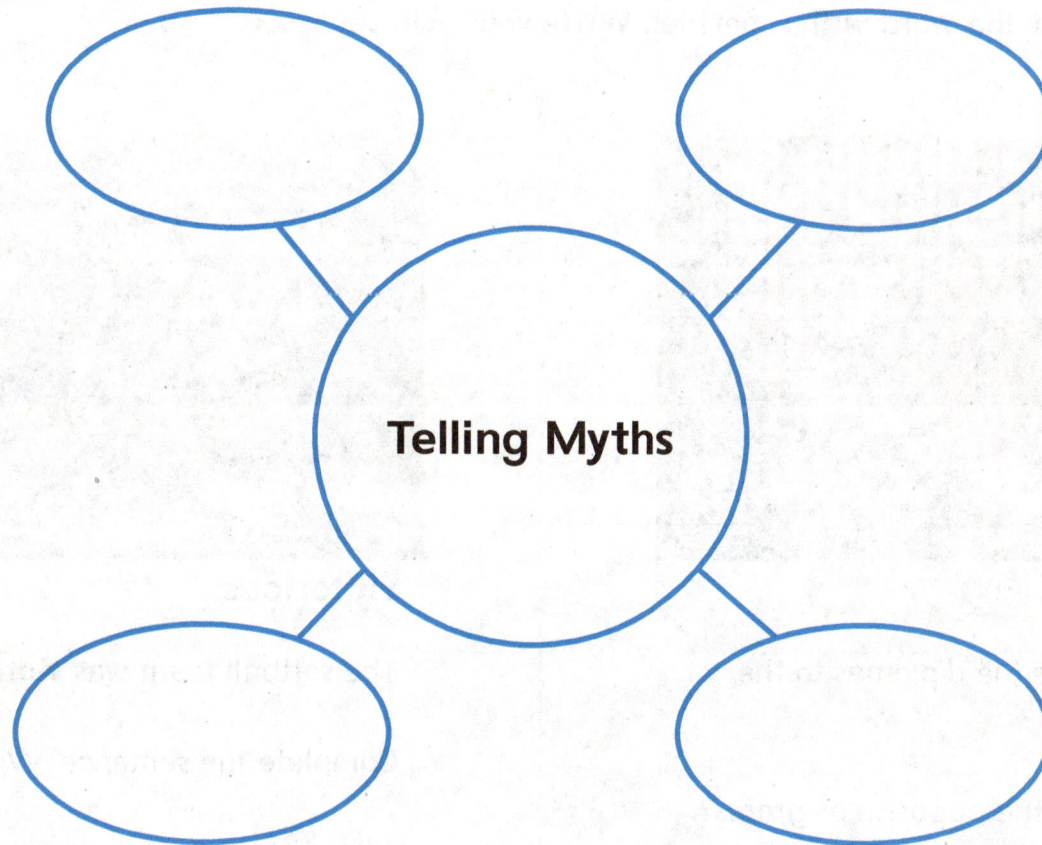

Telling Myths

Discuss the myth the actor is retelling. Use words from the chart. Complete the sentences.

The myth is about a Chinese _____. He is a _____ that people know about. He has a _____ face and a long,

black _____.

More Vocabulary

Image Source/Getty Images; Jupiterimages/Stockbyte/Getty Images

Look at the picture. Read the word. Then read the sentence. Talk about the word with a partner. Write your own sentence.

COLLABORATE

grants

The principal **grants** the diplomas to the students.

What word means the opposite of *grants*?

takes   **gives**   **does**

Who grants diplomas at your school?

_____ grants diplomas to students at my school.

victorious

The softball team was **victorious**.

Complete the sentence. Write the word.

After they won the game, the _____ softball team celebrated.

Name a victorious team.

_____ is a victorious team.

Words and Phrases: Suffixes *-ful* and *-less*

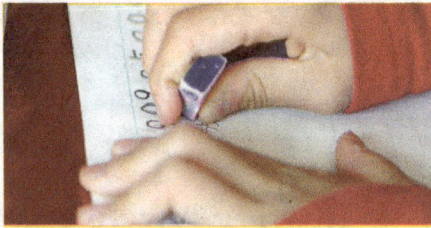

The suffix *-ful* means "full of."

use**ful** = full of use

What is useful?

An eraser is **useful**.

The suffix *-less* means "without."

form**less** = without form

What looks formless?

The clouds look **formless**.

COLLABORATE **Look at the picture. Read the sentence. Talk with a partner. Write the word that completes the sentence.**

The _____ cart holds many things.

    useful   **formless**

The spilled milk is _____.

    useful   **formless**

amana images inc./Alamy; ©Corbis; Image Source; Fuse/Getty Images

COLLABORATE

1 Talk About It

Look at the illustrations. Read the title and the introduction. Discuss what you see. Use these words.

snake   myth   struggle   creature

Write about what you see.

What do the title and introduction tell you?

The story is a _____

_____.

What does the illustration show?

The illustration shows _____

_____.

Take notes as you read the story.

THUNDER HELPER

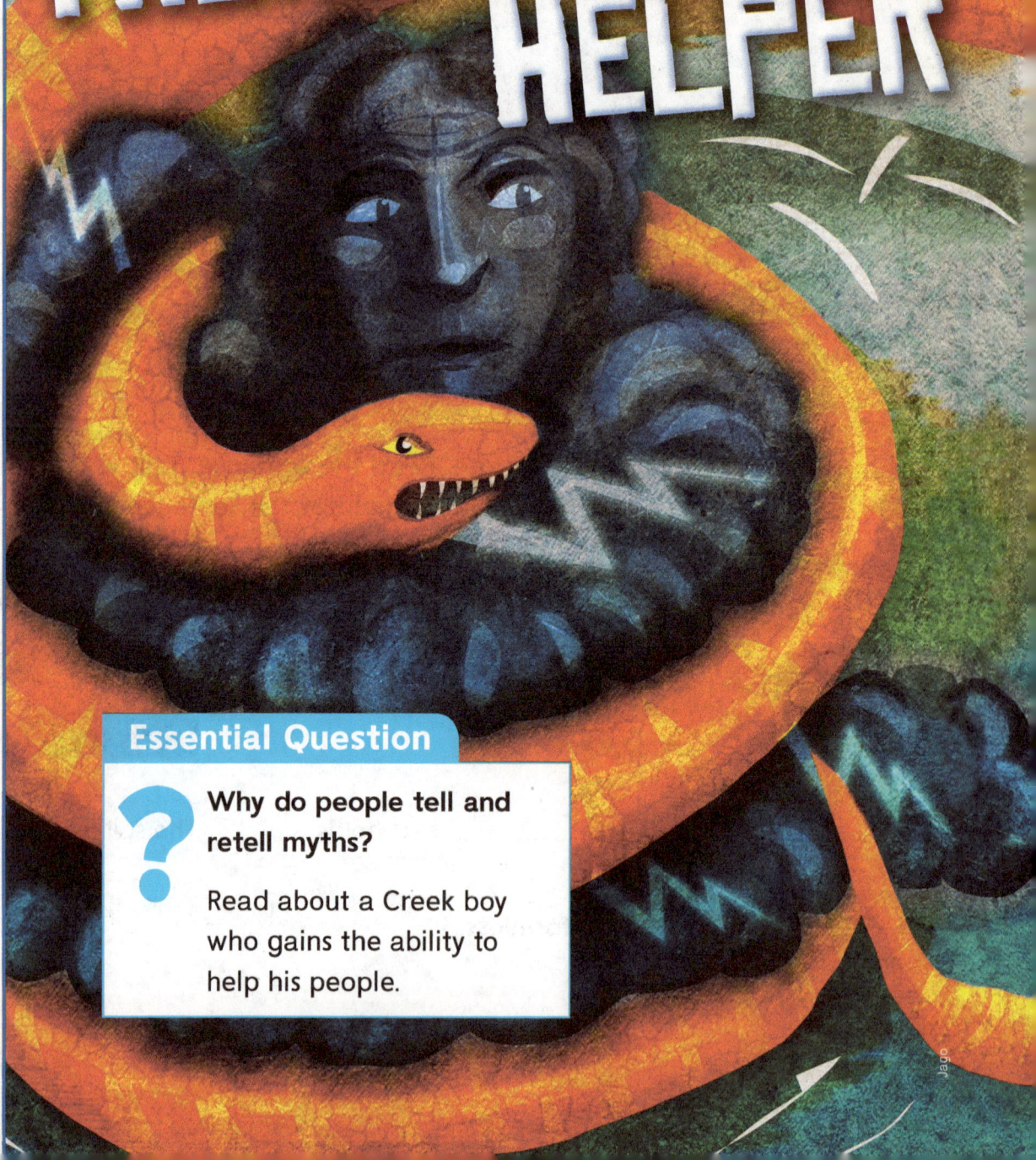

Essential Question

? **Why do people tell and retell myths?**

Read about a Creek boy who gains the ability to help his people.

The Creek are Native Americans who come from what are now Florida, Alabama, and Georgia. Their myths are passed down from generation to generation.

A boy from a small village always looked for ways to be useful to his people. One morning, he decided to catch fish in a nearby stream.

All at once, he heard a loud roar, so he crouched quickly, an arrow against his bow. The boy crept toward the rumbling until he reached the stream.

He saw two unearthly creatures high above the rushing water locked in a terrifying struggle. A dark and formless creature was the source of the booming roar. A fierce, wiry monster was coiled around the creature.

The boy remembered stories his people had told him. The boy recognized the monster. It was Tie-Snake, a trickster who drew people down into the desolate underworld. "But who is the shapeless one? Could it be Thunder himself?" the boy wondered, raising his bow.

1 Specific Vocabulary Ⓐ Ⓒ Ⓣ

Read the fourth paragraph. The word *unearthly* means "very strange and frightening." Underline the descriptions of the two unearthly creatures. What were these unearthly creatures doing?

These unearthly creatures were

locked _____.

2 Comprehension

Problem and Solution

Read the last paragraph. How does the boy figure out who the two creatures are? Circle two key sentences that tell you.

3 Sentence Structure Ⓐ Ⓒ Ⓣ

Reread the third sentence in the last paragraph. Underline the words that follow the comma. What is the purpose of these words?

The purpose of these words is to

_____ Tie-Snake.

① Comprehension
Problem and Solution

Read the third paragraph. How does the boy know which creature to believe? Underline the sentence that tells you.

COLLABORATE

② Talk About It

How did the boy become one of the best hunters in the village?

Thunder gave the boy _____

_____.

The boy worked hard to improve his

_____.

③ Specific Vocabulary Ⓐ Ⓒ Ⓣ

Read the last paragraph. Circle the word *deed*. What context clues help you understand the meaning of *deed*? Underline these clues. What will the boy's deed do?

The boy's deed will _____

_____.

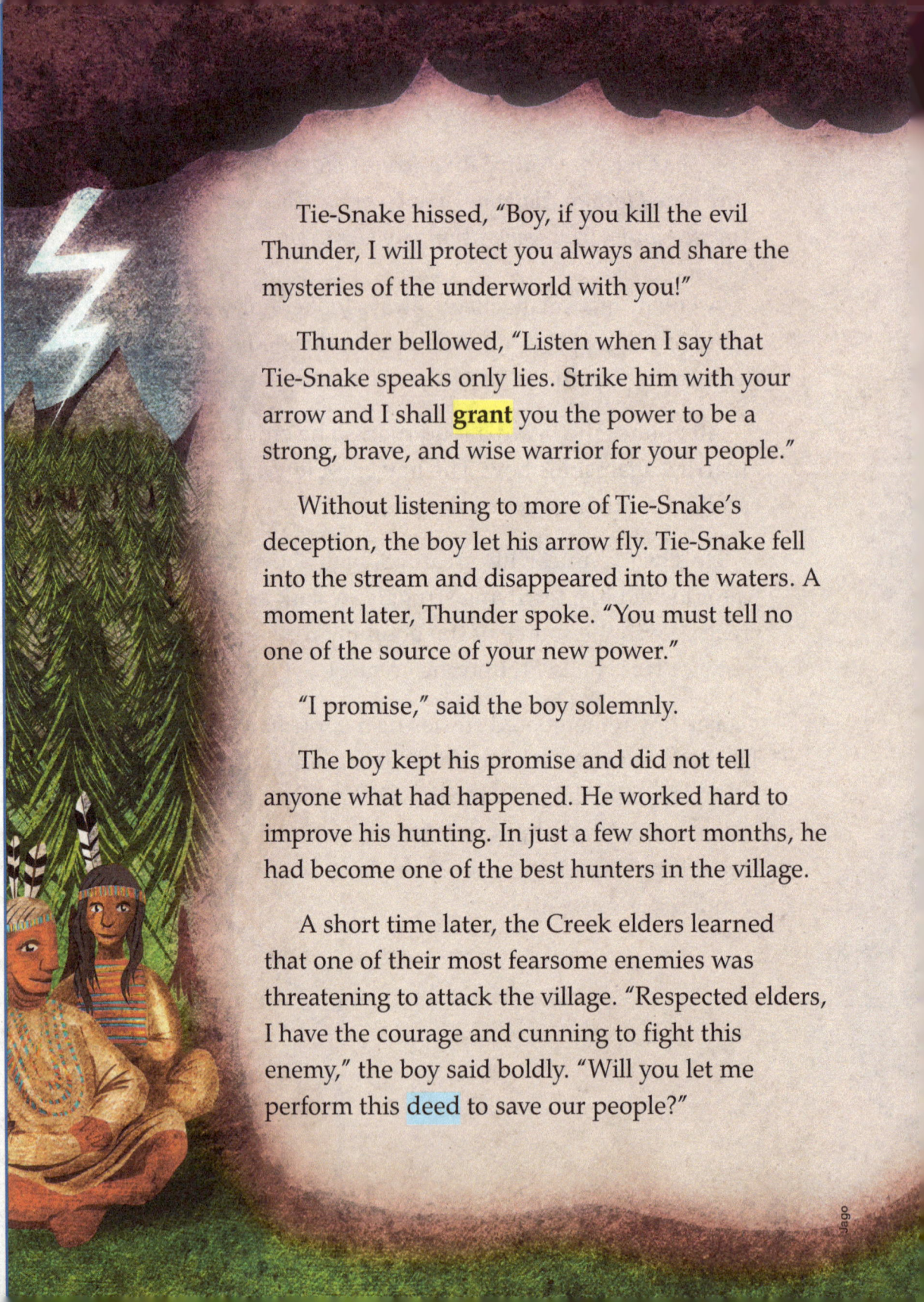

Tie-Snake hissed, "Boy, if you kill the evil Thunder, I will protect you always and share the mysteries of the underworld with you!"

Thunder bellowed, "Listen when I say that Tie-Snake speaks only lies. Strike him with your arrow and I shall grant you the power to be a strong, brave, and wise warrior for your people."

Without listening to more of Tie-Snake's deception, the boy let his arrow fly. Tie-Snake fell into the stream and disappeared into the waters. A moment later, Thunder spoke. "You must tell no one of the source of your new power."

"I promise," said the boy solemnly.

The boy kept his promise and did not tell anyone what had happened. He worked hard to improve his hunting. In just a few short months, he had become one of the best hunters in the village.

A short time later, the Creek elders learned that one of their most fearsome enemies was threatening to attack the village. "Respected elders, I have the courage and cunning to fight this enemy," the boy said boldly. "Will you let me perform this deed to save our people?"

Jago

Impressed by the boy's audacity, they agreed to let the boy fight their enemy. The chief declared, "You have proven your strength and bravery with your hunting. Now you must demonstrate your wisdom."

"I will not disappoint my people," the boy declared as he set off through the forest to face the enemy. The villagers gathered to await his return, but they grew somber as the hours passed. Suddenly, a deafening clap of thunder sounded, and a flash of lightning streaked through the sky. Moments later, smoke moved up and out through the trees. The people rejoiced because they knew that the boy had been victorious.

After the boy made his way out of the forest, the villagers celebrated his victory, and the elders called him *Menewa,* meaning "great warrior." From that day on, whenever the Creek heard Thunder, they knew that his helper Menewa was at work to keep their people safe.

Make Connections

? Talk about why the characters and plot of "Thunder Helper" would appeal to listeners generation after generation. ESSENTIAL QUESTION

Tell why a myth or story you know has special meaning to you. TEXT TO SELF

Text Evidence

1 Comprehension Problem and Solution

Reread the last paragraph on page 10 and the first paragraph on this page. Circle the problem the elders face. Underline the solution.

2 Sentence Structure A C T

Read the third sentence in the second paragraph. The conjunction *and* connects two complete ideas. Circle the word *and*. Underline the two ideas.

COLLABORATE

3 Talk About It

Did the boy use wisdom to defeat the enemy?

I think the boy _____ use wisdom to defeat the enemy.

I think he _____

_____.

That was _____ to do.

11

Respond to the Text

COLLABORATE **Partner Discussion** Work with a partner. Read the questions about "Thunder Helper." Show where you found text evidence. Write the page numbers. Then discuss what you read.

How did myths help the boy?

When the boy met Tie-Snake, the boy remembered _____.

Because the boy remembered Tie-Snake, _____

_____.

Text Evidence 🔍

Page(s): _____

Page(s): _____

What did the boy do in the middle part of the myth?

The boy trusted _____.

The boy defeated _____.

Text Evidence 🔍

Page(s): _____

Page(s): _____

How did the boy help his people at the end of the myth?

The boy worked hard and became _____.

The boy defeated the enemy because he had _____.

Text Evidence 🔍

Page(s): _____

Page(s): _____

COLLABORATE **Group Discussion** Present your answers to the group. Cite text evidence for your ideas. Listen to and discuss the group's opinions.

Write Work with a partner. Look at your notes about "Thunder Helper." Write your answer to the Essential Question. Use text evidence to support your answer. Use vocabulary words in your writing.

COLLABORATE

Why did the Creek people tell and retell myths?

The Creeks passed down myths from _____.

Because the boy remembered the stories of his people, _____

_____.

"Thunder Helper" shows what the Creek people think is important. In this myth, the boy is _____

_____.

The Creek people told myths over and over. These myths help people ____

_____.

Share Writing Present your writing to the class. Discuss their opinions. Talk about their ideas. Explain why you agree or disagree with their ideas. You can say:

COLLABORATE

I agree with _____.

That's a good comment, but _____.

Write to Sources

Erin

Take Notes About the Text I took notes on the sequence chart to answer the prompt: *Continue the dialogue between the boy and Tie-Snake in the story.*

pages 8–11

First
The boy recognized the monster.

Next
It was Tie-Snake, a trickster who drew people down into the desolate underworld.

Then
The boy raised his bow.

Last
Tie-Snake hissed, "Boy, if you kill the evil Thunder, I will protect you always and share the mysteries of the underworld with you!"

Write About the Text I used my notes from my sequence chart to write other things the boy and Tie-Snake might have said to each other.

"I do not believe you!" the boy said.

"Thunder is evil! You must help me!" Tie-Snake shouted. "I will give you wonderful things."

The boy shook his head. "You are a trickster. I cannot believe anything you say."

"Of course you can believe me," Tie-Snake said. "I will give you gold. I will give you a long life!"

TALK ABOUT IT

Text Evidence

Draw a box around a nickname for Tie-Snake that comes from the notes. How does this detail help Erin write an effective narrative?

Grammar

Circle the punctuation marks that show someone is speaking. Why did Erin use these marks?

Connect Ideas

Underline the last two sentences that tell what Tie-Snake promises the boy. How can you use the word *and* to connect the ideas?

Your Turn

Write what the boy and the elders might have talked about before the boy went to fight the enemy alone.

>> Go Digital!
Write your response online. Use your editing checklist.

15

Weekly Concept Personal Strength

? **Essential Question**
How do people show
inner strength?

>> *Go Digital*

What is the girl doing? Why does she need inner strength? How can she show inner strength? Write ways in the chart.

Inner Strength

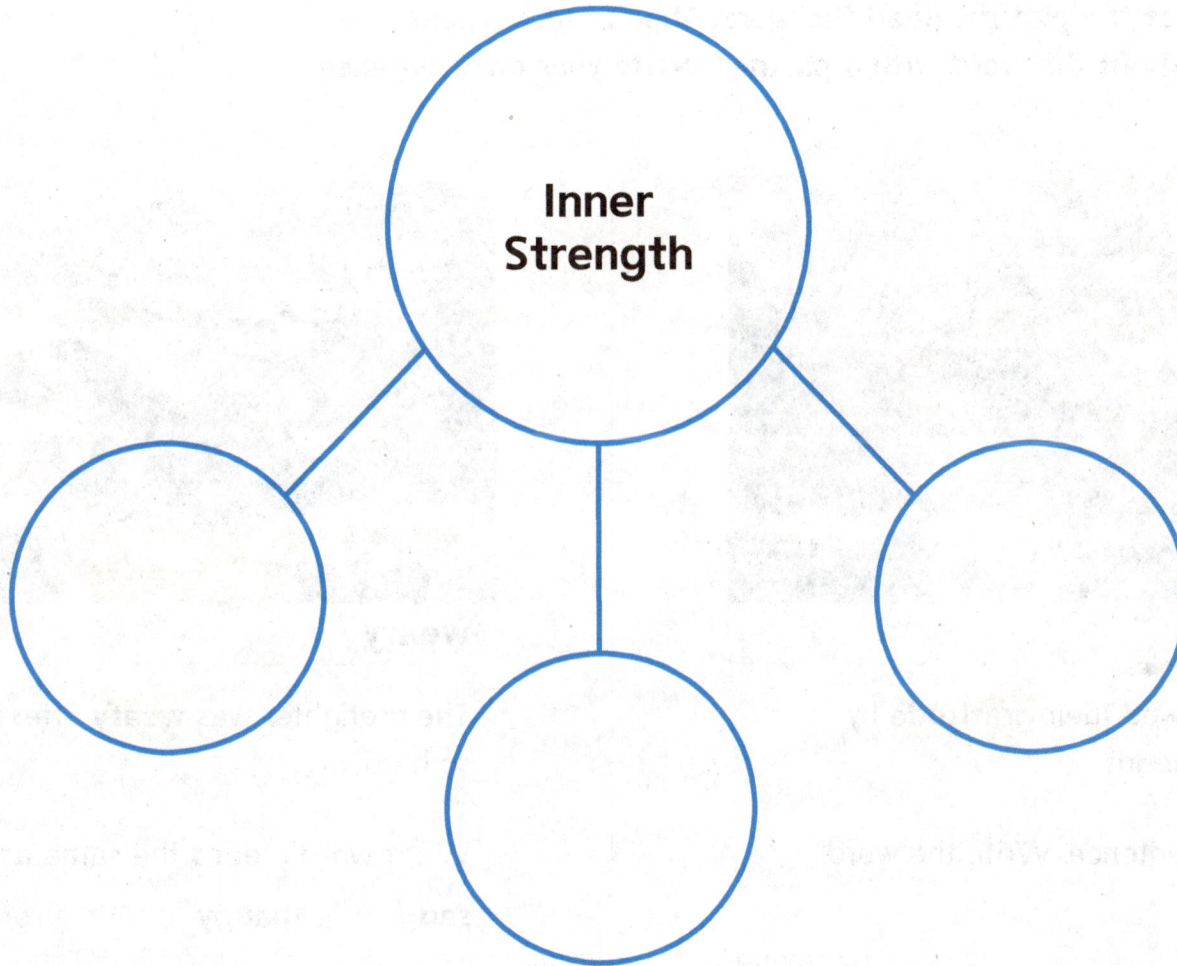

Discuss how the girl can show inner strength. Use words from the chart. Complete these sentences.

The girl can practice _____. The girl can try not to be

_____. The girl can perform _____.

Troy House/Corbis/Getty Images

More Vocabulary

COLLABORATE Look at the picture. Read the word. Then read the sentence. Talk about the word with a partner. Write your own sentence.

gratitude

The people showed their **gratitude** by clapping their hands.

Complete the sentence. Write the word.

You can show _____ by saying, "Thank you."

How do you show gratitude?

I show gratitude by _____

_____

_____.

weary

The firefighter was **weary** after working so hard.

What word means the same as *weary*?

sad   happy   tired

What makes you weary?

_____ makes me weary.

18

Words and Phrases: *and, but*

The word *and* combines two ideas.

Strawberries are red. Blueberries are blue.

Strawberries are red, **and** blueberries are blue.

The word *but* contrasts, or shows the difference between, two ideas.

Ripe tomatoes are red. Unripe tomatoes are green.

Ripe tomatoes are red, **but** unripe tomatoes are green.

COLLABORATE Talk with a partner. Look at the picture. Read the sentence. Write the word that completes the sentence.

Shona likes apples, _____ she does not like bananas.

        and   but

Jarron likes milk, _____ he likes juice.

        and   but

I. Rozenbaum & F. Cirou/PhotoAlto; Karol Franks/Moment Open/Getty Images; Tetra Images/Alamy; Steve Debenport/E+/Getty Images

COLLABORATE

1 Talk About It

Look at the illustration. Read the title. Discuss what you see. Use these words.

journey   daughter   freedom visitors

Write about what you see.

What does the title tell you?

The story is about _____

_____.

Who are the characters?

The characters are two _____

and a father and his _____.

Take notes as you read the story.

JOURNEY TO
Freedom

Essential Question

? **How do people show inner strength?**

Read about a girl who discovers her inner strength when she is asked to help people escape from slavery.

It is early summer 1851, and 12-year-old Abigail Parker is still finding her way after the death of her mother the previous winter. Her family has recently made their Massachusetts farm a station on the Underground Railroad, and now she and her father nervously await their first "delivery" of people on their way to Canada to escape slavery.

I could not sit for being so worried. Mother often said, "Patience is bitter, but its fruit is sweet." If only I possessed her calm.

"I see no sign of our four guests," Papa announced, raising my fears that they had met with misfortune. I heard a loud knock and my heart jumped.

Papa opened the door to find two **weary** women. He escorted the older woman to a chair. As they caught their breath, Papa asked, "Where are the others?"

"It's just Nellis and me," declared her companion, a girl. The older woman presented a letter, and I began to read: *"Dear Jonathan, I send you Nellis and Emma alone because their companions have fallen ill with fever. I hope you are able to shelter them temporarily. Respectfully, Jacob."*

Papa nodded, and I guided Nellis and Emma to the hiding place in the attic before wishing them a peaceful night.

Text Evidence

1 Specific Vocabulary Ⓐ Ⓒ Ⓣ

Read the first paragraph. The word *possessed* means "had." Why does Abigail wish she possessed her mother's calm?

If Abigail possessed her mother's

calf, she wouldn't _____

_____.

2 Comprehension
Cause and Effect

Read the first and second paragraphs. Why is Abigail worried? Underline the sentence that tells you.

Abigail is worried because she is

afraid that _____

_____.

3 Sentence Structure Ⓐ Ⓒ Ⓣ

Read the first sentence in the fourth paragraph. Which words show who is speaking? Underline these words. Which words show what the person says? Circle these words.

1 Comprehension
Cause and Effect

Read the third, fourth, and fifth paragraphs. Why does Abigail feel near fainting? What does her father say? Circle his words.

COLLABORATE

2 Talk About It

Reread the third paragraph. Why is getting a doctor a risk?

A doctor could report _____

_____,

and retaliation could be _____

_____.

3 Specific Vocabulary A C T

Read the last paragraph on this page. The word *determined* means "having a strong feeling that you are going to do something." Why was Abby determined to find the herb?

She was determined to find the

herb because _____.

In the morning, before I entered the attic, I couldn't help eavesdropping on the sound of choked coughing. Once inside, I shuddered when I saw Nellis's thin, pale face. "I fear it's the fever," she gasped.

I fetched Papa and pleaded: "She needs a doctor!"

"Think of the risk," he scolded. "A doctor could report us to the slave catchers, and retaliation could be dangerous. We must tend to this ourselves."

"Back in Virginia, I learned about some fever herbs," Emma said.

"Abby can get what you need," Papa suggested. I felt near fainting, but I listened carefully.

"Remember," Papa said to me, "the fields have eyes and the woods have ears, so be careful not to arouse suspicion."

I left with my basket, determined to find the herb Emma described. Finally, I spied the herb and plucked it, along with some mint leaves.

At home, Emma sorted through the leaves in the basket, handed me several, and told me to mince them finely. After Nellis drank the fever tea, she dozed off. Emma and I watched over her, and before long we fell to voicing our worries. I told her that I still missed Mother desperately. When Emma told me about the rigors of slavery, I could barely understand her fortitude. I confessed that I couldn't imagine being able to bear such hardship.

"It's why folks come together; problems shared are problems halved," said Emma smiling. "You'll have your mama's strength soon enough."

Nellis's fever broke that night. As Nellis and Emma prepared to continue their journey, they expressed their **gratitude** to Papa and me. I wished them safe passage and thanked Emma for helping me in my own journey.

Make Connections

? Talk about how Abby showed inner strength in finding the fever herb on her own. ESSENTIAL QUESTION

Describe a time when you discovered a personal strength that helped you do a difficult task. TEXT TO SELF

Text Evidence

1 Sentence Structure A C T

Read the first paragraph. Circle the pronoun *her* in the fifth sentence. Whom does *her* refer to? Underline the proper noun.

Her refers to _____.

COLLABORATE
2 Talk About It

Read the second paragraph. What does Emma mean when she says, "problems shared are problems halved"?

Emma means that when you share a problem with someone, your problems are less difficult to

_____.

3 Comprehension
Cause and Effect

Read the last paragraph. Why did Abby thank Emma at the end of the story? Underline the words that tell you.

Respond to the Text

Partner Discussion Work with a partner. Read the questions about "Journey to Freedom." Show where you found text evidence. Write the page numbers. Then discuss what you read.

What are Abby and her father doing at the beginning of the story?

Abby and her father are helping _____.

Text Evidence 🔍

Page(s): _____

What is Abby doing in the middle of the story?

Abby is worried about Nellis. At first, Abby wants to get a _____.

Instead, Abby searches for a _____.

Text Evidence 🔍

Page(s): _____

Page(s): _____

How does Abby feel about important events?

Abby is afraid of slave catchers, but she searches _____.

Emma tells Abby about _____.

Abby feels that slavery is a _____ that she couldn't bear.

Text Evidence 🔍

Page(s): _____

Page(s): _____

Page(s): _____

Group Discussion Present your answers to the group. Cite text evidence for your ideas. Listen to and discuss the group's opinions.

24

Write Work with a partner. Look at your notes about "Journey to Freedom." Write your answer to the Essential Question. Use text evidence to support your answer. Use vocabulary words in your writing.

How does Abby show inner strength during the story?

Abby and her father help _____.

Their work is dangerous. Someone could _____.

Abby searches for the fever herb even though _____

_____.

Abby shows inner strength when she _____

_____.

Share Writing Present your writing to the class. Discuss their opinions. Talk about their ideas. Explain why you agree or disagree with their ideas. You can say:

I agree with _____.

That's a good comment, but _____.

Write to Sources

Manuel

pages 20–23

Take Notes About the Text I took notes on the sequence chart to answer the prompt: *Write a letter from Jonathan to Jacob. Describe how Abby helped Nellis.*

First

Abby left with her basket to find the herb Emma described.

Next

She spied the herb and plucked it, along with some mint leaves.

Then

At home, Emma sorted through the leaves, and Abby minced them.

Last

Nellis drank the fever tea and dozed off.

Write About the Text I used my notes from my sequence chart to write a letter to Jacob.

Dear Jacob,

 Nellis and Emma arrived safely. But Nellis was ill with a fever by the next morning. Emma knew about some fever herbs that would help. My daughter Abby went out to find the herbs. She found the herbs. She collected a handful. Emma and Abby used the herbs to make fever tea for Nellis. She is feeling better now!

 Sincerely,

 Jonathan

TALK ABOUT IT

Text Evidence

Circle a sentence that comes from the notes and helps us learn about Abby. How does this detail help Manuel write the letter?

Letter

Draw a box around the greeting of the letter. What is the purpose of the greeting?

Connect Ideas

Underline the fifth and sixth sentences. How can you use the word *so* to combine the sentences?

Your Turn

Write a letter from Emma to the two companions left behind with Jacob. Describe what is happening at Jonathan's house.

>> Go Digital!
Write your response online. Use your editing checklist.

27

? Essential Question

How do people benefit from innovation?

>> *Go Digital*

COLLABORATE How is this new train different from older trains? How is it better?
Write ways in the chart.

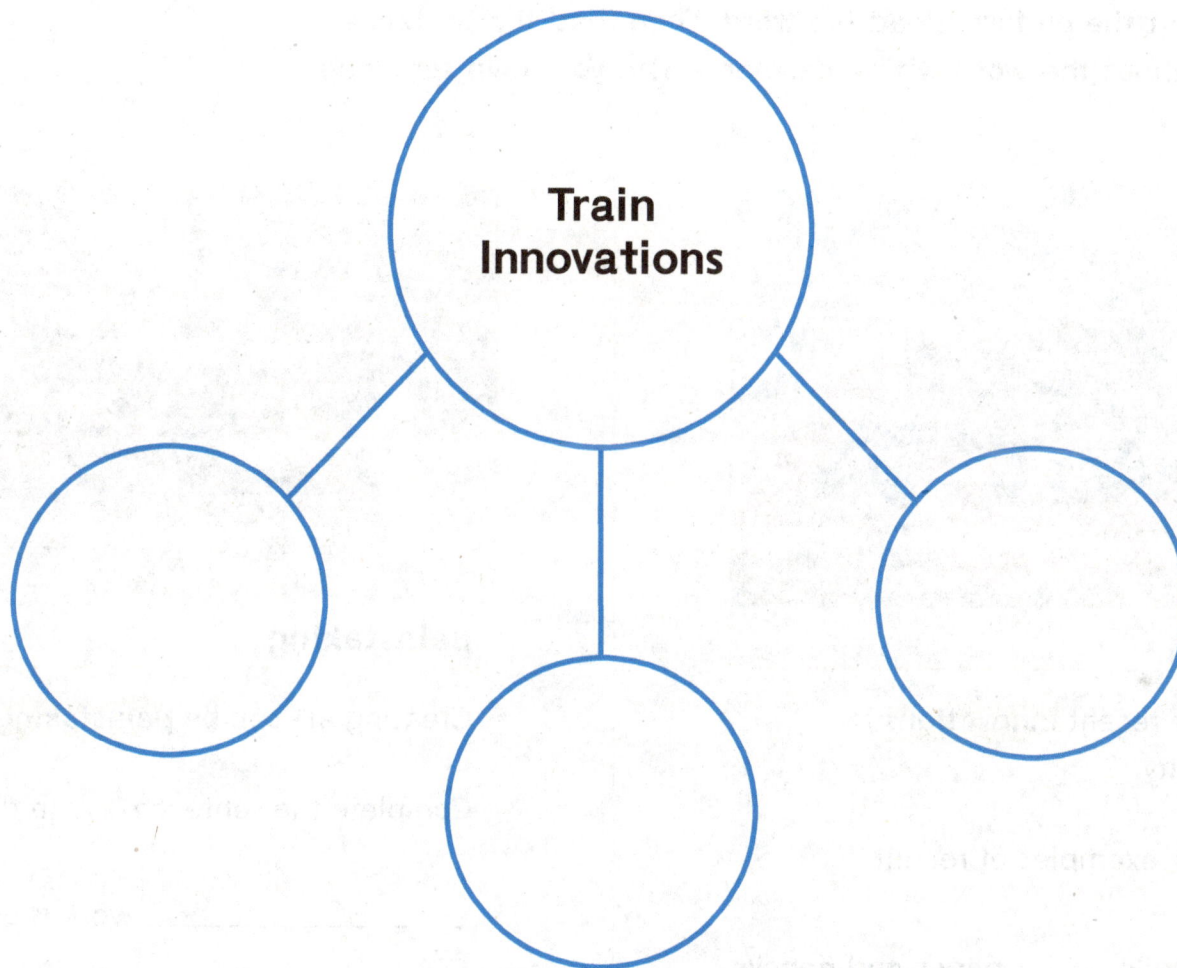

Train
Innovations

Discuss why the new train is better. Use words from the chart.
You can say:

The train has a new _____. This makes the train

_____. This also saves _____.

ELD.PI.6.1.Em, ELD.PI.6.2.Em, ELD.PI.6.5.Em, ELD.PI.6.10a.Em, ELD.PI.6.12a.Em, ELD.PII.6.1.Em, ELD.PII.6.6.Em, ELD.PII.6.7.Em See the California Standards section.

More Vocabulary

Look at the picture. Read the word. Then read the sentence.
Talk about the word with a partner. Write your own sentence.

innovations

Solar panels are recent **innovations** for making electricity.

What are other examples of recent *innovations*?

hammers and nails   **paper and pencils**

laptops and tablets

What are your favorite innovations?

My favorite innovations are _____

_____ .

painstaking

Creating art can be **painstaking**.

Complete the sentence. Write the word.

_____ work is usually difficult.

What thing is painstaking for you?

_____ is painstaking for me.

Words and Phrases: *larva* and *larvae*

The word *larva* is singular.

What do you see?

I see one **larva**.

The word *larvae* is plural.

What do you see?

I see three **larvae**.

COLLABORATE **Look at the picture. Read the sentence. Talk with a partner. Write the word that completes the sentence.**

There are many _____ on the leaves.

larva   larvae

There is one _____ on the boy's hand.

larva   larvae

U.S. Fish & Wildlife Service/Ryan Hagerty; Kelley Miller/National Geographic/Getty Images; Solina Images/Blend Images/Getty Images; Tono Balaguer/age fotostock

COLLABORATE

1 Talk About It

Look at the photographs and diagram. Read the title. Discuss what you see. Use these words.

science life cycle silk silkworm

Write about what you see.

What does the title tell you?

The text is about _____

_____.

What do you see in the photos and diagram?

The photos show _____

_____

_____.

The diagram shows _____

_____

_____.

Take notes as you read the text.

The Science of Silk

Essential Question

? **How do people benefit from innovation?**

Read how innovations in silk production have made this cloth available to many people.

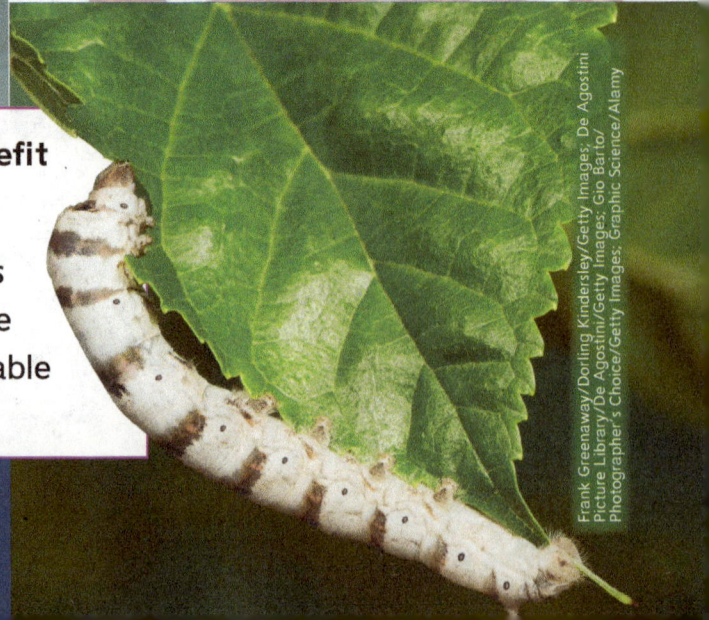

Frank Greenaway/Dorling Kindersley/Getty Images; De Agostini Picture Library/De Agostini/Getty Images; Gio Barto/ Photographer's Choice/Getty Images; Graphic Science/Alamy

Five thousand years ago in China, silk was a rare and expensive luxury. But people have engaged in the manipulation of the silk-making process. Now, silk is relatively inexpensive and used by many people. Technology and innovations have changed the way silk is made.

A Better Silkworm

Bombyx mori is a special moth typically used to produce silk. The moth's life cycle has four stages: egg, larva, pupa, and adult. Silk is the material that the larva produces to make its cocoon.

Bombyx mori is a hybrid. People bred the moth over many years to make it strong and productive. A *Bombyx mori* moth lays about 500 eggs, more than other silkworm species. Many of these eggs develop into healthy larvae that grow very quickly.

The *Bombyx mori* is unable to fly. It relies entirely on humans to feed its larvae mulberry leaves. Humans must also make sure that the eggs are kept at a specific temperature.

Silkworm Life Cycle

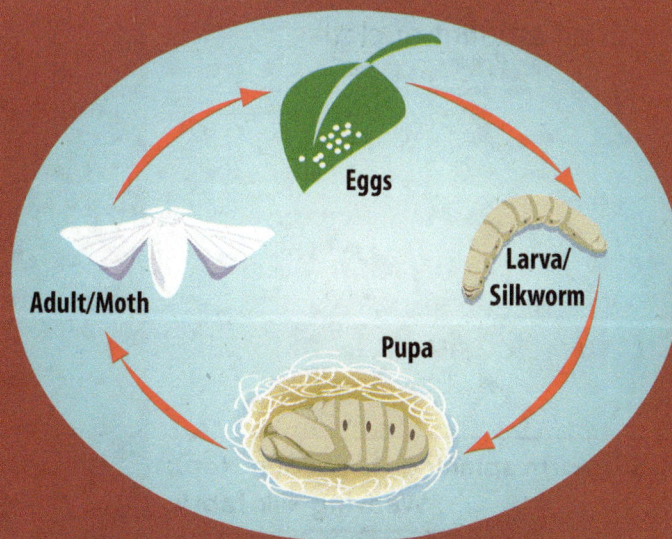

Eggs

Larva/Silkworm

Pupa

Adult/Moth

Text Evidence

1 Sentence Structure A C T

Read the last sentence in the second paragraph. Circle the word *larva* in the adjective clause. Underline the verb *produces*. What material does the larva produce to make its cocoon?

The larva produces _____

to make its _____.

2 Specific Vocabulary A C T

Read the third paragraph. The word *productive* means "producing, or making, a lot of something." In what way is the *Bombyx mori* moth productive? Underline the sentence that tells you.

3 Comprehension
Cause and Effect

Read the fourth paragraph. What is an effect of the *Bombyx mori* moth not being able to fly? Underline the sentence that tells you.

❶ Comprehension
Cause and Effect

Read the first paragraph. Why do people work hard to raise the *Bombyx mori* moth? Underline the sentence that tells you.

❷ Specific Vocabulary Ⓐ Ⓒ Ⓣ

Read the third paragraph. The word *unwind* means "unwrap something that is wrapped around an object." How do people unwind the cocoons?

They unwind the cocoons without

breaking _____

_____ .

COLLABORATE

❸ Talk About It

What parts of the ancient process of raising silkworms do people still use today?

They harvest and _____ .

They unwind _____ .

They twist _____ .

People work hard to raise the *Bombyx mori* because its silk is strong. It can absorb more dye than other types of silk. The round, smooth filaments create a fine, luminous (shiny) cloth.

From Cocoon to Thread

For thousands of years, raising silkworms was an important part of Chinese culture. Women and girls tended the worms, processed the cocoons, spun the thread, and weaved the silk. These painstaking chores took many hours per day. They produced beautiful results but only a small amount of cloth.

People who raise silkworms still use parts of the ancient, or old, process. They harvest cocoons and soften the cocoons in water. Carefully, they unwind the cocoons without breaking the long, delicate silk filament. They twist the filaments together into thread.

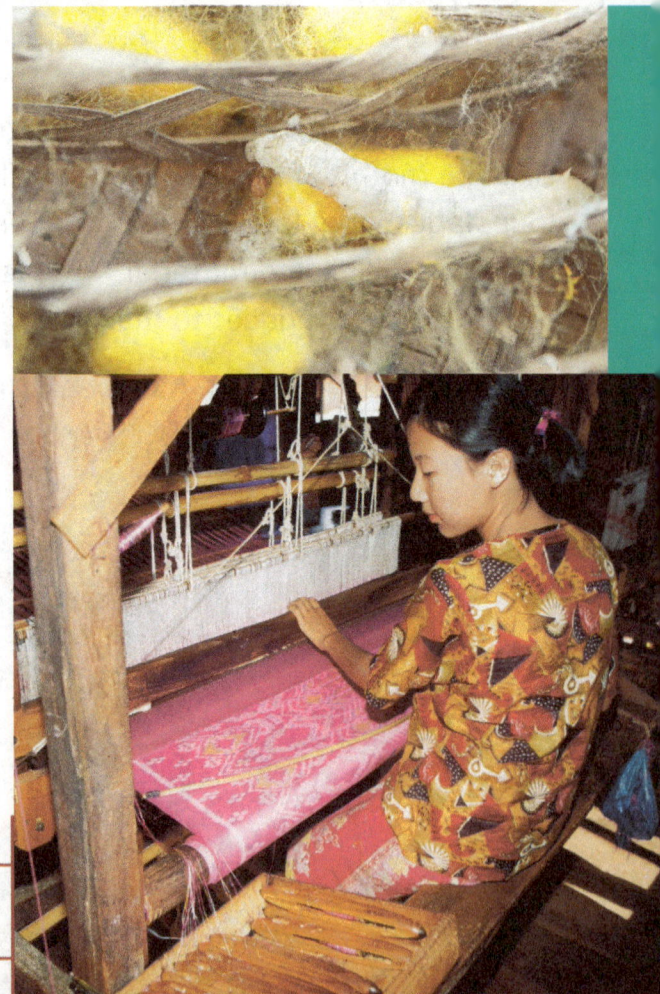

Silkworm spinning its cocoon (top); Weaving silk fabric

(t) Olga Khoroshunova/Alamy; (c) Praweena/iStock/360/Getty Images; (b) Travel Ink/Gallo Images/Getty Images

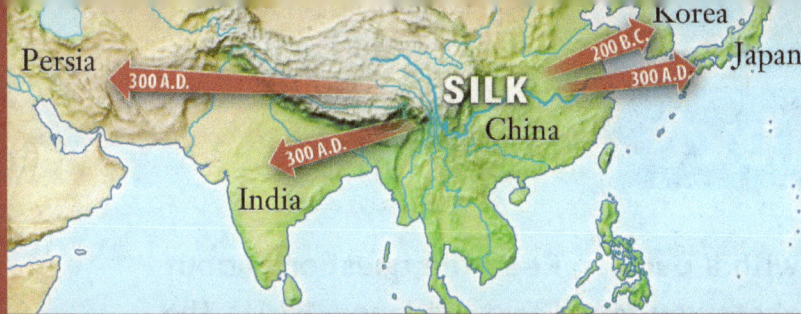

A secret for 3,000 years, Chinese silk farming spread to Korea about 200 B.C. Then it spread to India, Japan, and Persia about 300 A.D.

Advances in Silk Technology

China kept the process for making silk a secret for centuries. Eventually, the silkworm eggs were smuggled out of China. Once people understood the process, they tried to improve upon it.

The French invented the reeling machine. This machine made it easier to unwind the cocoons. Then they invented the Jacquard loom. This loom allowed weavers to create complex designs. More recently, industrial weaving machines started to produce large amounts of silk cloth quickly.

All of these advances meant more silk products could be made at a lower cost.

Today, China remains the leading producer of silk. But the demand for silk reaches far beyond China's borders. For this reason, people will continue seeking better ways to produce silk.

Make Connections

? Talk about the role humans play in silk production. How have innovations over time benefitted people? **ESSENTIAL QUESTION**

What other technology have you learned about that developed through innovation over time? How has this technology helped you? **TEXT TO SELF**

RedChopsticks/Getty Images

Text Evidence

1 Specific Vocabulary ACT

Read the first paragraph. The verb *smuggled* means "took someone or something from one country to another illegally." Why did the people smuggle the silkworm eggs out of China? Circle the sentence that tells you.

2 Sentence Structure ACT

Read the last sentence of the first paragraph. The conjunction *once* means "from a certain time." What did people do once they understood the process? Circle the part of the sentence that tells you.

COLLABORATE

3 Talk About It

Why is silk available to many people today?

People found ways to make silk

_____ and _____.

Two ways are the _____

and the Jacquard _____.

Respond to the Text

Partner Discussion Work with a partner. Read the questions about "The Science of Silk." Show where you found text evidence. Write the page numbers. Then discuss what you learned.

How did the *Bombyx mori* moth change silk making?

The *Bombyx mori* moth lays _____.

Text Evidence 🔍 Page(s): _____

The silk from the *Bombyx mori* moth is _____.

Page(s): _____

The *Bombyx mori* moth changed silk making because its silk is _____

_____.

Page(s): _____

How did technology change silk making?

Text Evidence 🔍

People invented _____.

Page(s): _____

Now people can produce _____

_____.

Page(s): _____

The cost of making silk products _____.

Page(s): _____

Group Discussion Present your answers to the group. Cite text evidence for your ideas. Listen to and discuss the group's opinions.

Write Work with a partner. Look at your notes about "The Science of Silk." Write your answer to the Essential Question. Use text evidence to support your answer. Use vocabulary words in your writing.

How did people benefit from innovations in silk making?

The *Bombyx mori* moth lays many eggs. Many of the eggs develop into

_____.

The silk that comes from the *Bombyx mori* moth is better than the silk from other moths. The silk makes a fine _____.

Machines made the process _____.

With these innovations, people could _____

_____.

Share Writing Present your writing to the class. Discuss their opinions. Talk about their ideas. Explain why you agree or disagree with their ideas. You can say:

I agree with _____.

That's a good comment, but _____.

Write to Sources

Take Notes About the Text I took notes on the main idea and details chart to answer the question: *How does the* Bombyx mori *silk moth improve the silk-making process?*

pages 32–35

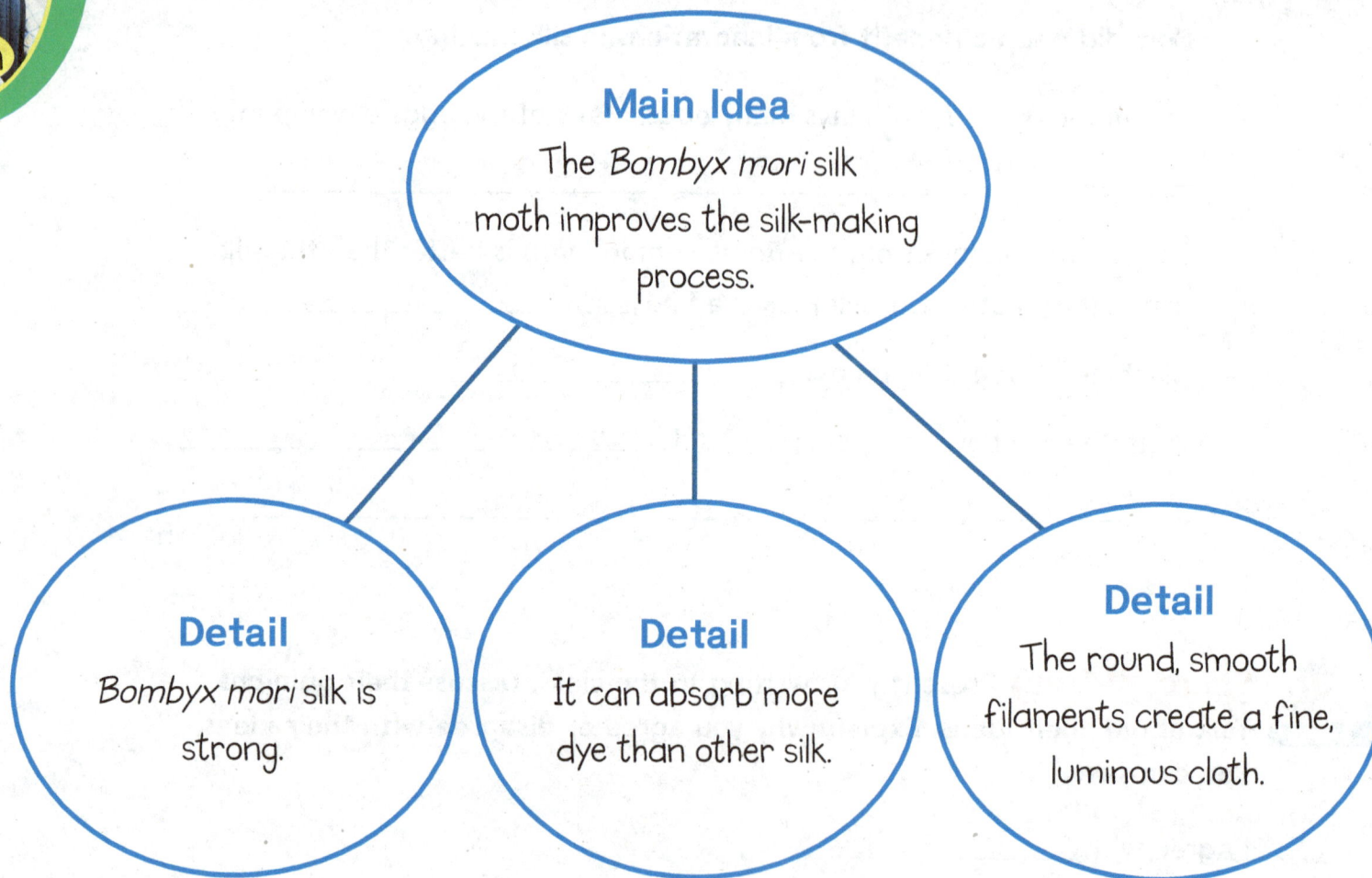

Main Idea
The *Bombyx mori* silk moth improves the silk-making process.

Detail
Bombyx mori silk is strong.

Detail
It can absorb more dye than other silk.

Detail
The round, smooth filaments create a fine, luminous cloth.

Write About the Text I used my notes from my main idea and details chart to write a paragraph about *Bombyx mori* silk.

Student Model: *Informative Text*

The *Bombyx mori* is a type of moth. This moth is used to make silk. This silk moth improves the silk-making process. First, *Bombyx mori* silk is strong. Second, *Bombyx mori* silk can absorb more dye. This helps create colorful silk cloth. Third, the *Bombyx mori* filament is round and smooth. So, the cloth is finer and more luminous than other silk.

TALK ABOUT IT

COLLABORATE

Text Evidence

Underline a detail sentence that comes from the notes. Why did Roshan use this information as a supporting detail?

Grammar

Draw a box around the words that connect the supporting details. Why did Roshan use these connecting words?

Condense Ideas

Circle the first and second sentences. How can you use the word *that* to combine the sentences to condense ideas?

Your Turn

COLLABORATE

How have inventions improved silk production?

>> *Go Digital*
Write your response online. Use your editing checklist.

?

Essential Question

How does technology lead to discoveries?

>> *Go Digital*

What does the photo show? How was the picture taken? What did scientists learn? Write words in the chart.

Technological Breakthroughs

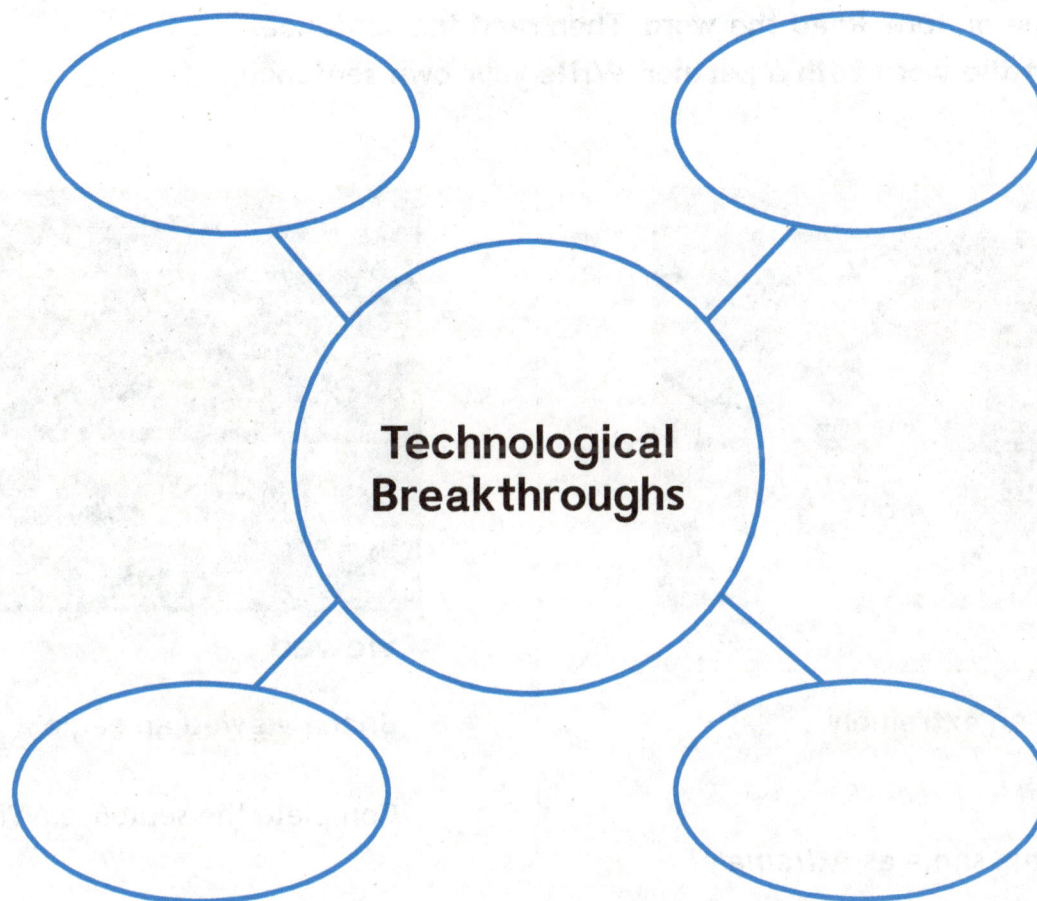

Discuss how the camera helped scientists learn. Use words from the chart. Complete these sentences.

The camera helped scientists learn about the _____.

Scientists learned about the galaxy's curving _____.

Scientists also learned about the _____ in the blue regions.

More Vocabulary

Look at the picture. Read the word. Then read the sentence.
Talk about the word with a partner. Write your own sentence.

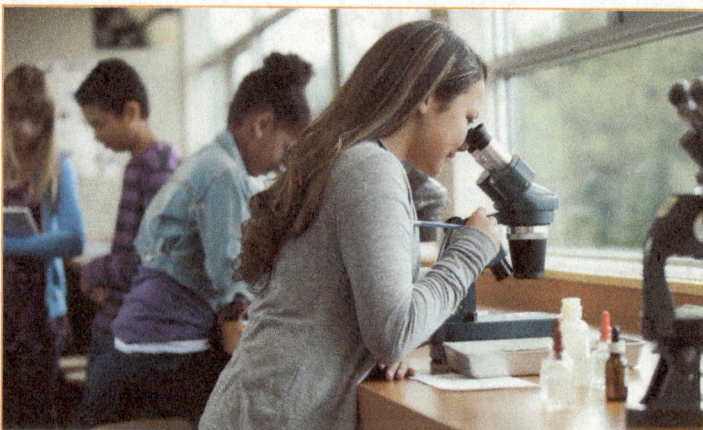

extremely

Armani is looking at an <mark>extremely</mark> small object.

What word means the same as *extremely*?

very　　　**quickly**　　　**slowly**

What makes you <mark>extremely</mark> happy?

_____ makes

me extremely happy.

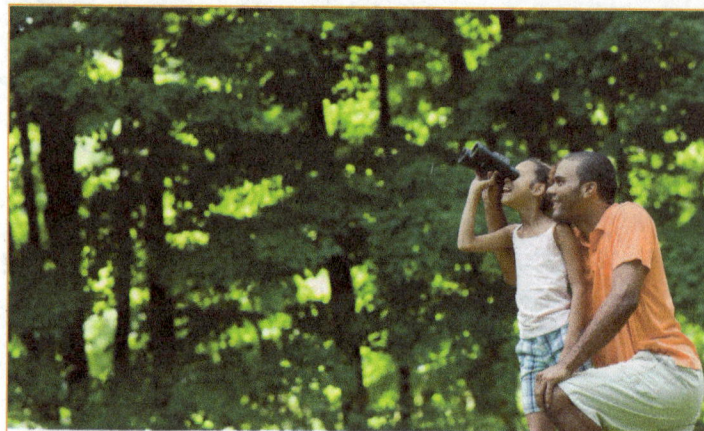

viewed

Briana <mark>viewed</mark> an eagle.

Complete the sentence. Write the word.

I was excited when I _____ the

magic show.

What interesting thing have you <mark>viewed</mark>?

I viewed _____.

Words and Phrases: Multiple-Meaning Words

A *bank* is a place for keeping money.

Where is the woman putting her money?

She is putting her money in the **bank**.

A *bank* is also a group of objects in a row.

What is in the library?

A **bank** of tables is in the library.

COLLABORATE **Look at the picture. Read the sentence. Talk with a partner. Circle the meaning of the underlined word.**

This building has a <u>bank</u> of elevators.

place for keeping money

group of objects in a row

The woman is at the <u>bank</u>.

place for keeping money

group of objects in a row

COLLABORATE

1 Talk About It

Look at the photograph. Read the title and the caption. Discuss what you see. Use these words.

astronomers   **night**   **sky**

Write about what you see.

This text is about _____

_____.

What does the photograph show?

The photograph shows the _____

_____.

What do "light detectives" do?

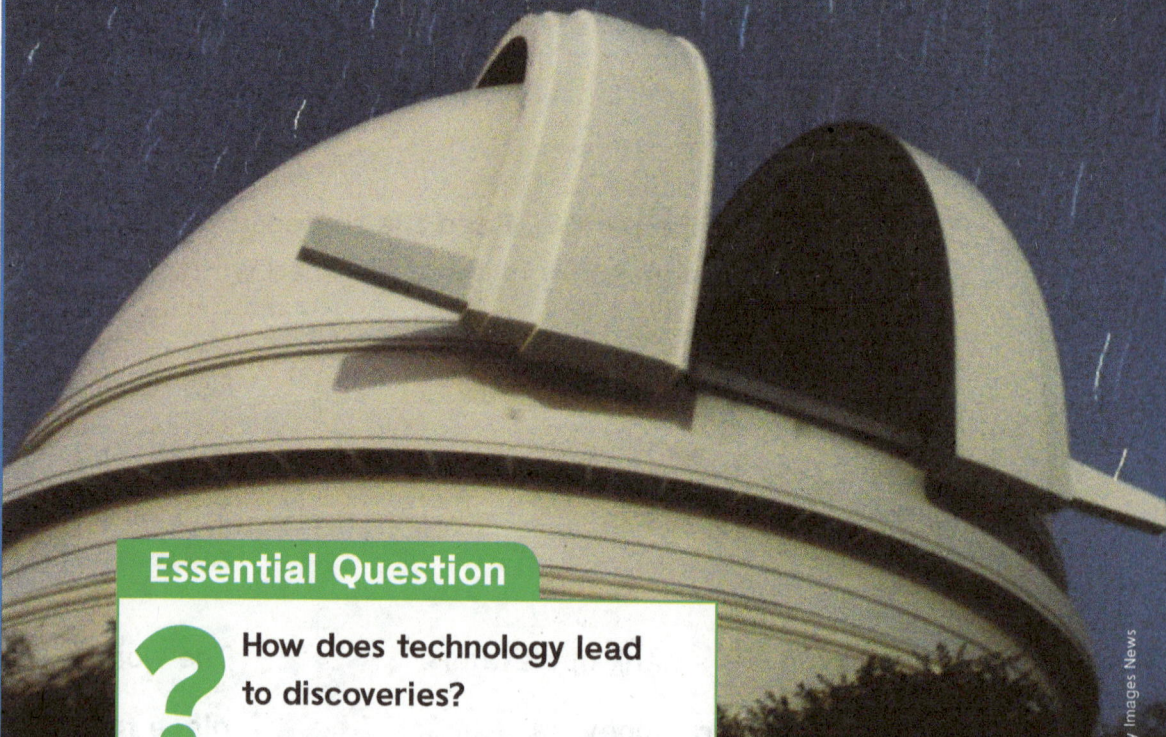

They search _____

_____.

Take notes as you read the text.

Light
Detectives

Essential Question

?

How does technology lead to discoveries?

Read about astronomers and the technology they use to find distant objects in our solar system.

Palomar Observatory, California

Sandy Huffaker/Stringer/Getty Images News

Astronomers use technologies to study the light that we see reflected off the most distant objects in our solar system. These scientists are "light detectives" who collect clues about our solar system.

Discovering Pluto

In the 1920s, astronomers noticed something strange. The outer planets seemed to be affected by an unexplained force. Was there another planet out there with a gravitational pull strong enough to tug on Uranus and Neptune? To find this object, a young scientist named Clyde Tombaugh perfected a method for searching the sky.

Tombaugh used a new telescope at the Lowell Observatory in Arizona. He took photographs of the night sky and then ==viewed== these images in a machine called a blink comparator. This tool superimposed two images of the same area taken at different times, placing one on top of the other. It blinked back and forth between the two images. Tombaugh could see if any objects had changed position from one time period to the next. In 1930, he discovered Pluto.

The Kuiper Belt

In 1992, astronomers identified a disk-like region that extended up to 9.3 billion miles from the sun. They named it the Kuiper Belt, after Gerard Kuiper who had theorized the existence of such a region. Astronomers estimated there were about 70,000 large, icy objects in the Kuiper Belt. Were some even larger than Pluto?

Text Evidence

❶ Comprehension
Sequence

Read the second paragraph. What happened before Clyde Tombaugh perfected a method for searching the sky? Underline the sentences that tell you.

❷ Sentence Structure ⒶⒸⓉ

Read the second sentence of the third paragraph. Whom does the pronoun *he* refer to? Circle the proper noun in the first sentence.

❸ Specific Vocabulary ⒶⒸⓉ

Read the third paragraph. Circle the context clues that help you understand the meaning of *superimposed*. What did the superimposed images show?

The superimposed images showed if any objects had _____

_____.

1 Sentence Structure ACT

Read the last sentence in the first paragraph. What two objects do the robots control? Underline the words that tell you. Then write them below.

_____

2 Specific Vocabulary ACT

Reread the first paragraph. The word *repeated* means "done again and again." What are astronomers taking repeated images of?

Astronomers are taking repeated

images of _____.

COLLABORATE

3 Talk About It

What was important about the bright object discovered in 2003?

The bright object was _____

_____.

Using New and Old Data

To answer the question, astronomer Michael Brown and his colleagues used a similar method to Tombaugh's blink comparator. But they took advantage of new technology. Like Tombaugh, Brown's team takes repeated images of the night sky. Robots control both the telescope and its camera.

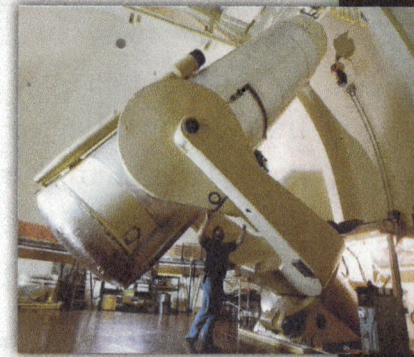

Oschin Telescope, Palomar Observatory

Instead of using a blink comparator, Brown's team sends the images to a bank of ten computers at the California Institute of Technology (CIT). The computers superimpose images taken at different times and identify objects that are possibly moving. Then the team studies the data to try to verify the movement. In 2003, the team discovered a bright shape that was moving more slowly than any known object in our solar system. Could this be the object tugging on Uranus and Neptune?

1 A 161-megapixel camera mounted on the telescope.

2 Multiple images of the night sky.

3 CIT computers superimpose images.

4 Astronomers Mike Brown, Chad Trujillo, and David Rabinowitz analyze data.

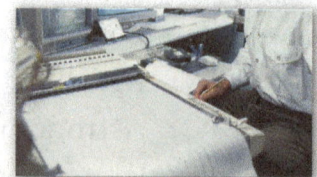

Astronomers eventually named the object Eris. But its super-slow speed posed a problem. Brown calculated that Eris takes 560 years to orbit the sun. So it would take many years to confirm that Eris affects planetary orbits. Brown decided to check photos taken by other astronomers. Luckily, Eris appeared in photographs taken as early as 1950. By combining these images with current data, the team developed a more complete view of Eris's size and movements.

The team estimated that Eris was 25 to 40 percent more massive than Pluto. They used pictures taken by the Hubble Space Telescope to confirm this estimate. They found out they were wrong. Eris is only slightly larger than Pluto. Eris has an **extremely** reflective surface. The bright, reflected light makes Eris look larger than it really is.

Both Pluto and Eris were classified as "dwarf planets," rather than planets. Astronomers predict that new technology will allow them to identify several more dwarf planets in the Kuiper Belt.

The Moon

Earth

Pluto

Eris

Relative sizes of Earth, the Moon, Pluto, and Eris

NASA

Make Connections

? Talk about the technology astronomers have used to study distant objects in our solar system. **ESSENTIAL QUESTION**

Describe a time you used a tool, such as a ruler, calculator, or camera, to answer a question. **TEXT TO SELF**

Text Evidence 🔍

1 Sentence Structure Ⓐ Ⓒ Ⓣ

Read the second and third sentences in the first paragraph. Underline the sentence that gives the cause. Circle the sentence that gives the effect.

2 Comprehension Sequence

Read the first paragraph. Michael Brown calculated that Eris takes 560 years to orbit the sun. What did he do after that? Underline the sentence that tells you.

3 Specific Vocabulary Ⓐ Ⓒ Ⓣ

Read the last paragraph. *Classified* means "arranged into a group or groups." How did astronomers classify Pluto and Eris?

Astronomers classified Pluto and

Eris as _____.

Respond to the Text

Partner Discussion Work with a partner. Read the questions about "Light Detectives." Show where you found text evidence. Write the page numbers. Then discuss what you learned.

How did technology help Clyde Tombaugh?

Clyde Tombaugh used a blink comparator to _____.

Tombaugh could see if any objects had _____.

Tombaugh discovered _____.

Text Evidence 🔍

Page(s): _____

Page(s): _____

Page(s): _____

How does technology help Michael Brown and his team?

Today, Michael Brown and his team use _____

_____

Michael Brown and his team discovered _____.

Technology helped astronomers classify Pluto and Eris as _____

_____

Text Evidence 🔍

Page(s): _____

Page(s): _____

Page(s): _____

Group Discussion Present your answers to the group. Cite text evidence for your ideas. Listen to and discuss the group's opinions.

Write Work with a partner. Look at your notes about "Light Detectives." Write your answer to the Essential Question. Use text evidence to support your answer. Use vocabulary words in your writing.

COLLABORATE

How does technology lead to discoveries about our solar system?

Using a blink comparator, Clyde Tombaugh compared _____
_____.

Tombaugh saw that objects had _____.

He also discovered _____.

Michael Brown and his team discovered Eris using _____
_____.

Technology leads to discoveries about our solar system because _____
_____.

Share Writing Present your writing to the class. Discuss their opinions. Talk about their ideas. Explain why you agree or disagree with their ideas. You can say:

COLLABORATE

I agree with _____.

That's a good comment, but _____.

Write to Sources

Inez

Take Notes About the Text I took notes on the sequence chart to answer the question: *How does new technology help scientists find moving objects in space?*

pages 44–47

First
Michael Brown and his team take repeated images of the night sky.

Next
Robots control both the telescope and its camera.

Then
Brown's team sends the images to a bank of computers at the California Institute of Technology.

Last
The computers superimpose images taken at different times and identify objects that are possibly moving.

Write About the Text I used my notes from my sequence chart to write an informative paragraph about new technology that takes pictures of the night sky.

Student Model: *Informative Text*

Michael Brown and his team use new technology to find moving objects in space. They start by taking repeated images of the night sky. Robots control both the telescope and its camera. Scientists don't have to be there all night long. Then scientists send the images to computers at the California Institute of Technology. The last step is for computers to superimpose the images by laying one on top of the other. That way, scientists can see which objects moved. Most things they find are not big discoveries, but some are exciting.

TALK ABOUT IT

COLLABORATE

Text Evidence

Draw a box around a sentence about robots that comes from the notes. Why did Inez use this information as a supporting detail?

Grammar

Circle a word or phrase that connects events. Why did Inez use this connecting word or phrase?

Connect Ideas

Underline the third and fourth sentences. How can you use the word *so* to connect the sentences?

Your Turn

COLLABORATE

What events led to the discovery of Eris?

>> *Go Digital!*
Write your response online. Use your editing checklist.

? **Essential Question**

How have tools used for exploration evolved over time?

›› Go Digital

What does the photo show? How does this tool help the scientist explore? Write words in the chart.

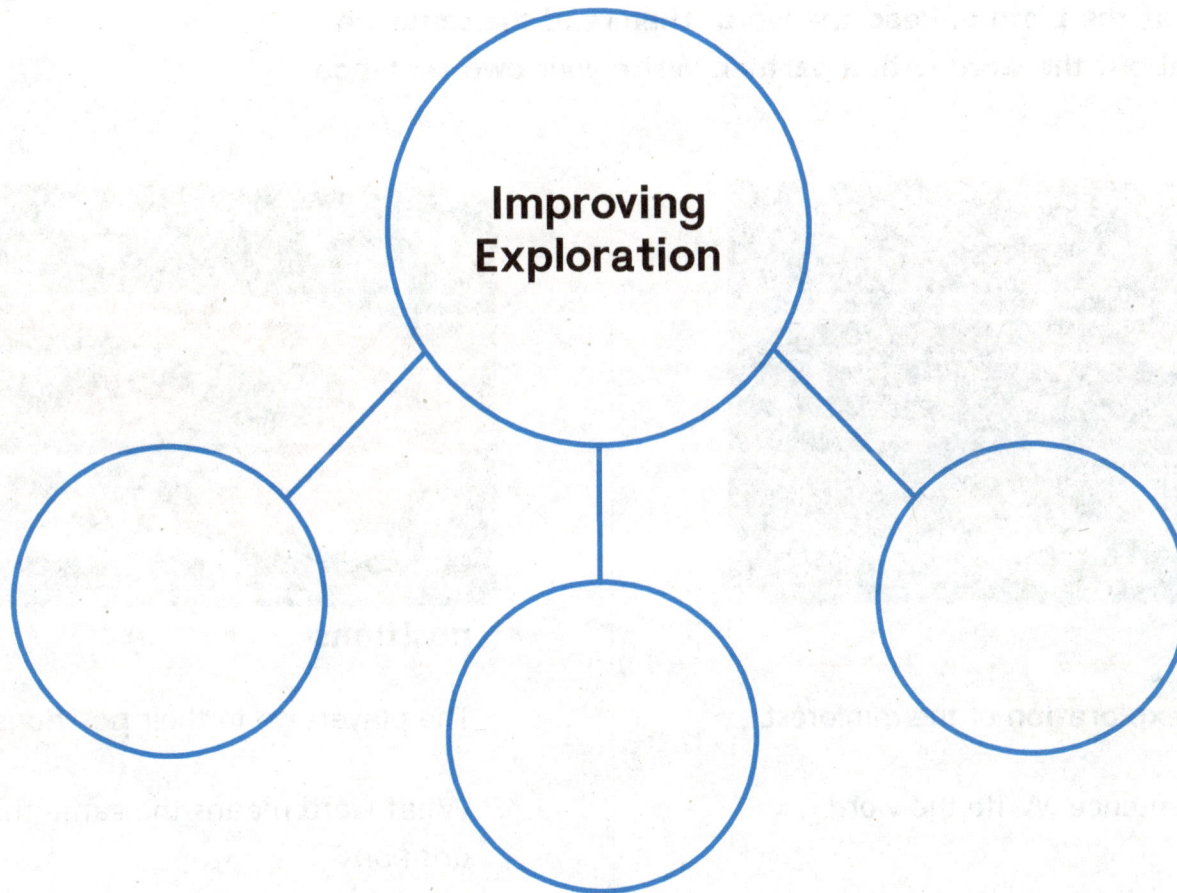

Improving
Exploration

Discuss why the scientist likes this new tool. Use words from the chart. Complete these sentences.

The _____ is a new tool for the scientist. The scientist

can explore in shallow _____ and get close to

_____.

More Vocabulary

Look at the picture. Read the word. Then read the sentence.
Talk about the word with a partner. Write your own sentence.

exploration

Jamie is on an **exploration** of the rainforest.

Complete the sentence. Write the word.

An _____ is like an adventure.

What kind of exploration would you like to go on?

I would like to go on an exploration of

_____ .

positions

The players go to their **positions**.

What word means the same thing as
positions?

times   **places**   **names**

When do the players go to their positions?

The players go to their positions _____

_____ .

Eyecandy Images/Getty Images Plus/Getty Images; jpinlac/Moment/Getty Images

Words and Phrases: Multiple-Meaning Words

The noun *aid* means "something that helps."

What is a calculator?

A calculator is an **aid** with math problems.

The verb *aid* also means "to help."

What will the people do?

The people will **aid** the whale.

COLLABORATE Look at the picture. Read the sentence. Talk with a partner. Underline the correct meaning of the word *aid*.

Billy uses crutches as an *aid*.

something that helps   **to help**

The fireman will *aid* the kitten.

something that helps   **to help**

COLLABORATE

1 Talk About It

Look at the photographs. Read the title and the captions. Discuss what you see. Use these words.

tools   explorers   sailor   sea

Write about what you see.

This text is about _____

_____

_____.

What do the photographs show?

The photographs show _____

_____

_____.

Take notes as you read the text.

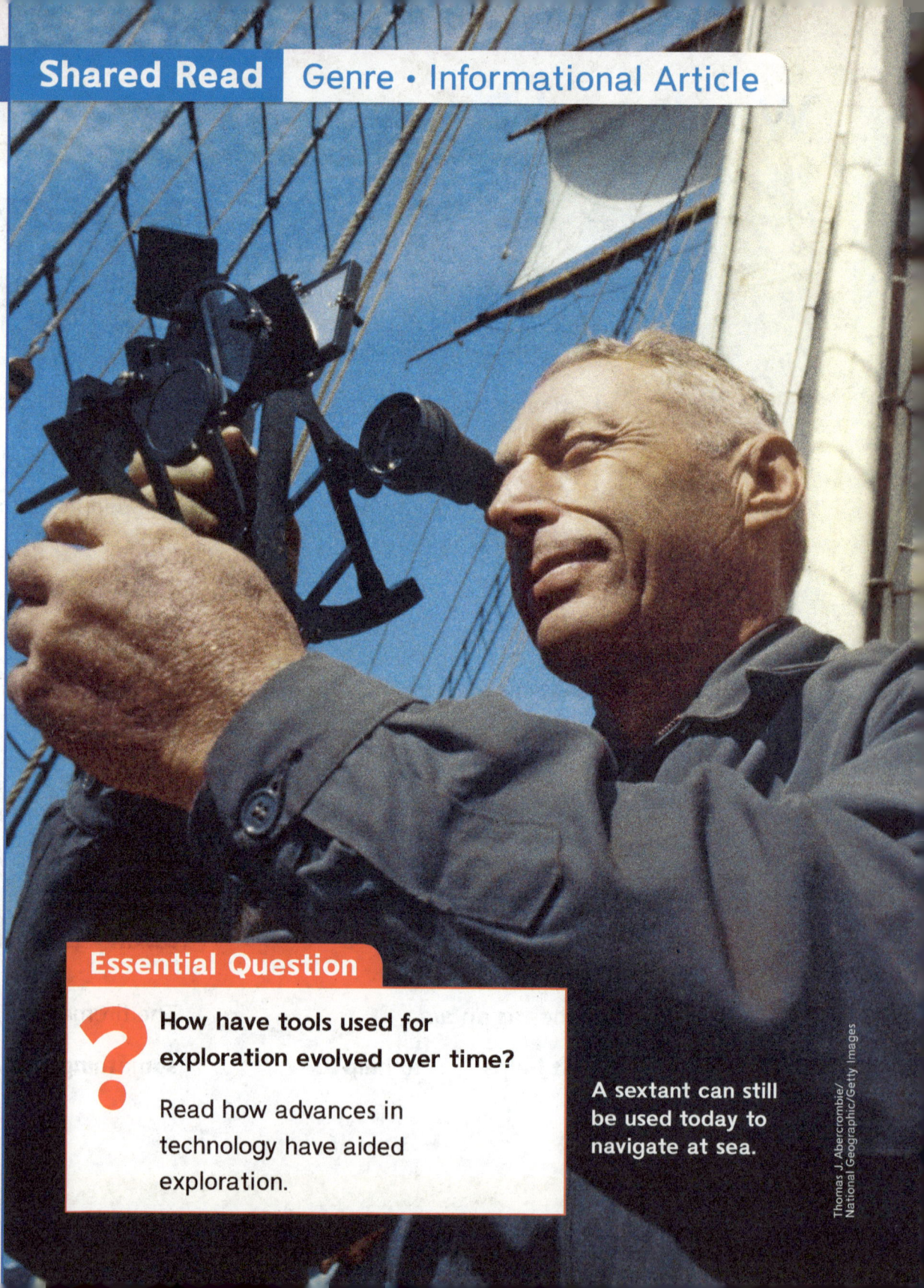

Essential Question

? **How have tools used for exploration evolved over time?**

Read how advances in technology have aided exploration.

A sextant can still be used today to navigate at sea.

Thomas J. Abercrombie/
National Geographic/Getty Images

Tools of the Explorer's Trade

The following survey of several historical navigation techniques shows how technologies evolve over time.

The North Star

Sailors of early civilizations used the star Polaris, or the North Star, to find their positions at sea. But using Polaris for navigation had problems. First, it can only be seen on clear nights. Second, Polaris can only be seen from the Northern Hemisphere. Using the North Star was a good choice at certain times, but something better was needed.

The Astrolabe

The astrolabe was an advanced measuring tool invented in the Middle East. Though its primary application was to make computations about time and the **positions** of the Sun, Moon, planets, and stars, the astrolabe was employed as a technological aid to navigation. It gave mariners a way to determine the latitude of their ships.

A Moorish astrolabe made in Andalusia, Spain

(t) A. Gómez/Flickr/Getty Images; (bkgd) Jeff Spielman/Photodisc/Getty Images

Text Evidence

1 Sentence Structure A C T

Read the first sentence of the second paragraph. Circle the commas. What part of the sentence gives extra information about the star Polaris? Underline this part. Then write it.

2 Comprehension
Author's Point of View

Read the second paragraph. What is the author's point of view about using the North Star for navigation? Underline the two sentences that tell you.

3 Specific Vocabulary A C T

Read the third paragraph. The word *employed* means "used." How did mariners employ the astrolabe?

Mariners employed the astrolabe to figure out _____

_____.

Text Evidence 🔍

❶ Sentence Structure ⒶⒸⓉ

Read the second sentence. Circle the pronoun *it*. What does the pronoun refer to? Underline the noun phrase in the first sentence.

❷ Specific Vocabulary ⒶⒸⓉ

Read the last sentence in the first paragraph. Circle the word that helps you understand the meaning of *modern*. How is the sextant used with modern technologies?

With modern technologies, the

sextant is used as _____

_____.

❸ Talk About It

Why is a compass a useful tool for explorers?

A compass shows direction by using

_____.

A compass can be used in all

_____.

The Sextant

The sextant also used the positions of the Sun and stars to find a location on Earth. Developed in Asia Minor in the late tenth century, it was used to measure the angle between a celestial object and the horizon. When navigators studied this measurement, they could find their ship's location on a nautical chart. The sextant is still used today as a backup to modern technologies.

The Compass

The compass is made by balancing a magnetic needle above a circular dial. Earth's strong magnetic field causes the needle to swing into a north-south position. Because a compass indicates direction in all weather and at all times of the day or night, explorers recognized its importance as a navigational tool. Historians are unsure who invented the compass. But we do know it was in use in China as early as the eleventh century.

A compass uses Earth's magnetic field to show direction.

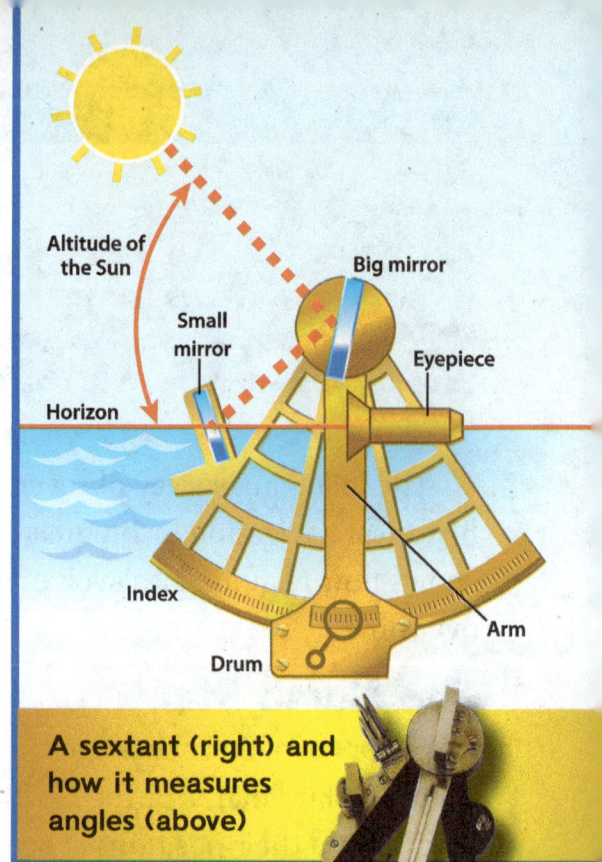

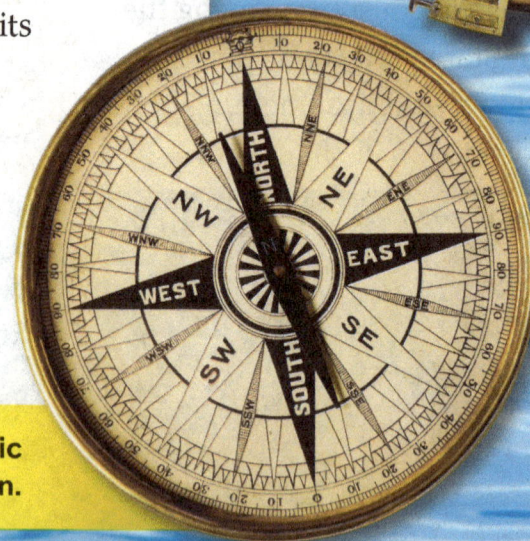

Altitude of the Sun

Big mirror

Small mirror

Eyepiece

Horizon

Index

Arm

Drum

A sextant (right) and how it measures angles (above)

An Opinion: Let's Keep Looking

Exploration takes courage and creative resourcefulness. For most of history, exploration was limited to Earth's surface. But in 1930, we began diving into the ocean's depths. In 1969, we landed on the moon. The probes that we deployed into deep space in 1977 are still sending valuable data back to us. Today, robotic vehicles survey the surface of Mars, and we have a powerful telescope in orbit that sends us spectacular photographs of the formation of distant stars.

Exploration fuels our inventiveness and inspires our imaginations. We are constantly raising our aspirations. Modern technologies provide more and better tools to explore remote places. When it comes to exploration, the best is yet to come. We should continue to value and encourage curiosity.

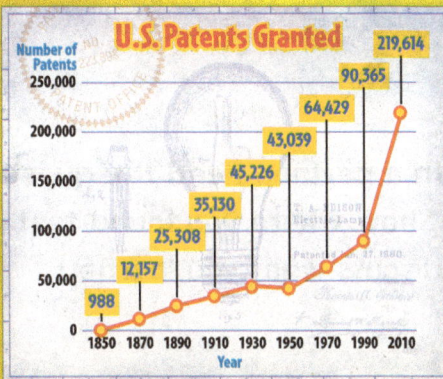

U.S. Patents Granted

Number of Patents

250,000

200,000

150,000

100,000

50,000

0

988 · 12,157 · 25,308 · 35,130 · 45,226 · 43,039 · 64,429 · 90,365 · 219,614

1850 1870 1890 1910 1930 1950 1970 1990 2010

Year

(bkgd) Jeff Spielman/Photodisc/Photodisc/Getty Images; (t) NASA and The Hubble Heritage Team (AURA/STScI) ; (b) Stocktrek Images/Getty Images

Inventing as Fast as We Can

When the U.S. government grants patents to "promote the Progress of Science and useful Arts," it gives exclusive rights to inventors for a set period of time. The number of patents issued in the years from 1850 to 2010 reveals a stunning increase in the rate of technological innovations.

Make Connections

Talk about how technologies used for exploration have developed over time. **ESSENTIAL QUESTION**

Tell how a technological tool you use helps you learn about your community and the world. **TEXT TO SELF**

Text Evidence

1 Specific Vocabulary A C T

Read the first paragraph. The word *formation* means "creation." How are we able to see the formation of distant stars? Circle the words that tell you.

2 Comprehension
Author's Point of View

Read the second paragraph. What is the author's point of view about the future of exploration? Underline the sentence that tells you.

COLLABORATE

3 Talk About It

What tools help us explore Mars?

_____ help us survey the surface of Mars.

A _____

sends us photographs of _____

_____.

59

Respond to the Text

Partner Discussion Work with a partner. Read the questions about "Tools of the Explorer's Trade." Show where you found text evidence. Write the page numbers. Then discuss what you learned.

What did early civilizations use to navigate?

Text Evidence 🔍

Sailors of early civilizations used _____.

Page(s): _____

But this method was used only _____.

Page(s): _____

So explorers needed _____.

Page(s): _____

What other tools did explorers use to navigate?

Text Evidence 🔍

To find a location on Earth, navigators used _____ and _____.

Page(s): _____

These tools helped navigators find a location on Earth at night by using _____.

Page(s): _____

The compass could be used at any time because it used _____.

Page(s): _____

Group Discussion Present your answers to the group. Cite text evidence for your ideas. Listen to and discuss the group's opinions.

Write Work with a partner. Look at your notes about "Tools of the Explorer's Trade." Write your answer to the Essential Question. Use text evidence to support your answer. Use vocabulary words in your writing.

COLLABORATE

How have tools used for exploration evolved over time?

Sailors of early civilizations used the North Star, but _____

_____.

New tools, such as the sextant and astrolabe, used _____

_____.

After the compass was invented, explorers located position in all _____

_____.

Tools used for exploration evolved as explorers needed _____

_____.

Share Writing Present your writing to the class. Discuss their opinions. Talk about their ideas. Explain why you agree or disagree with their ideas. You can say:

COLLABORATE

I agree with _____.

That's a good comment, but _____.

Write to Sources

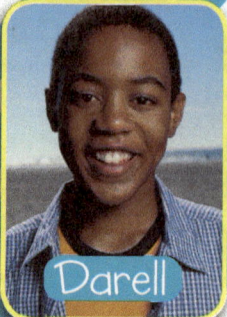

Darell

pages 56–59

Take Notes About the Text I took notes on the idea web to answer the question: *Is the fast rate of technological inventions good or bad?*

Detail

Technological inventions help us communicate with people near and far.

Detail

New technologies help us explore remote places and learn about space.

Main Idea

Technological inventions are good.

Detail

Today, robotic vehicles study the surface of Mars.

Detail

Someday, we might get to travel to Mars and communicate with Earth.

Student Model: *Argument*

I think that the fast rate of technological inventions is good. Some people get upset when a new computer is outdated in a year. That kind of change can be frustrating. But, technological inventions are good, too. They help us communicate with people near and far. New technologies also help us explore remote places and learn about space. Today, robotic vehicles study the surface of Mars. Someday we might get to travel to Mars. On Mars, we might communicate with people on Earth. The fast rate of technological inventions makes amazing things possible within our lifetime!

TALK ABOUT IT

COLLABORATE

Text Evidence

Draw a box around a detail that comes from the notes. Why did Darell use this detail to support his argument?

Grammar

Circle a connecting word that provides a detail about time. Why did Darell use this word?

Connect Ideas

Underline the three sentences about Mars. How can you use the word *but* or *and* to connect two of the sentences?

Your Turn

COLLABORATE

Which early tool used by navigators was the most important invention?

>> *Go Digital!*
Write your response online. Use your editing checklist.